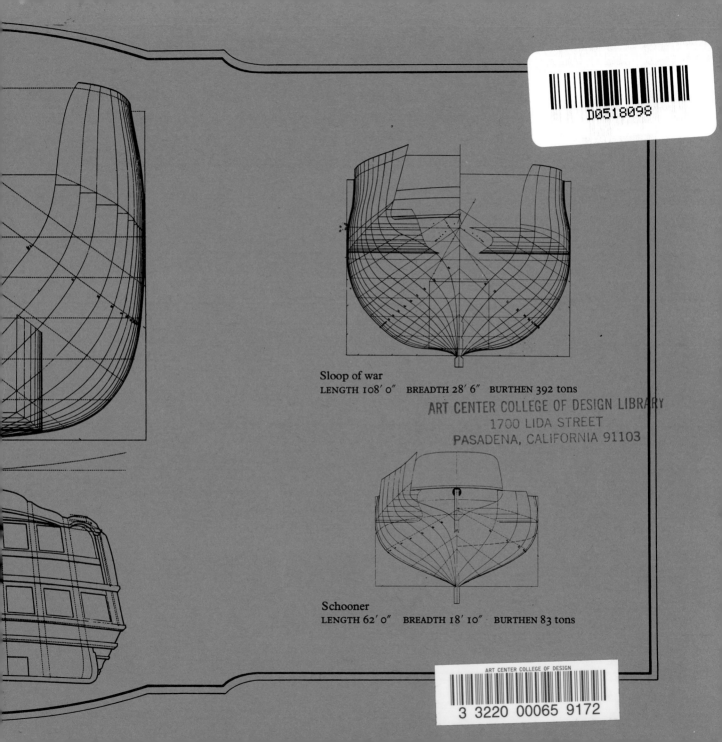

Sloop of war
LENGTH 108′ 0″   BREADTH 28′ 6″   BURTHEN 392 tons

Schooner
LENGTH 62′ 0″   BREADTH 18′ 10″   BURTHEN 83 tons

(front cover) An Indiaman in a Fresh
Breeze, C. Brooking, 1723-1759. The
Indiaman is shown lying-to with her
headsails backed, awaiting the pilot
boat perhaps.

(back cover) A Vice-Admiral of the Red
with his squadron c 1755, C. Brooking
1723-1759. The two-decker is wearing
the flag of a Vice-admiral of the Red.
On the right is a ketch-rigged bomb
vessel, distinctive with her main mast
set well back to give the heavy mortars
a clear field of fire. The ketch still has
the lateen mizzen, unlike the larger
vessels in which, at this period, the
mizzen sail had become quadrilateral
and was set completely abaft the
mizzen mast.

All the illustrations are from material
in the National Maritime Museum at
Greenwich, to the Trustees of which
I am indebted for permission to
reproduce in this volume. I am
indebted also to my colleagues in the
Museum with whom I have discussed
many of the topics touched upon here.

© Crown Copyright 1980
First published 1980

ISBN 0 11 290314 2

Designed by HMSO Graphic Design

Printed in England for
Her Majesty's Stationery Office
by W. S. Cowell Ltd, Ipswich

Dd 696315   K160

National Maritime Museum

THE SHIP

The Century before Steam

The Development of the Sailing Ship

1700–1820

Alan McGowan

London
Her Majesty's Stationery Office

Contents

70 gun ship in a light breeze, *c* 1750,
C. Brooking 1723–1759. A typical
3rd Rate of the mid-18th century. The
differing angle of the yards suggests
that she has just altered course and that
the crew is in process of trimming the
sails accordingly. The two small vessels
are cutters.

Introduction by the General Editor

This is the fourth of a series of ten short books on the development of the ship, both the merchant vessel and the specialised vessel of war, from the earliest times to the present day, commissioned and produced jointly by the National Maritime Museum and Her Majesty's Stationery Office.

The books are each self-contained, each dealing with one aspect of the subject, but together they cover the evolution of vessels in terms which are detailed, accurate and up-to-date. They incorporate the latest available information and the latest thinking on the subject, but they are readily intelligible to the non-specialist, professional historian or layman.

Above all, as should be expected from the only large and comprehensive general historical museum in the world which deals especially with the impact of the sea on the development of human culture and civilisation, the approach is unromantic and realistic. Merchant ships were and are machines for carrying cargo profitably. They carried the trade and, in the words of the very distinguished author of the second book in this series, 'the creation of wealth through trade is at the root of political and military power'. The vessel of war, the maritime vehicle of that power, follows and she is a machine for men to fight from or with.

It follows from such an approach that the illustrations to the series are for the most part from contemporary sources. The reader can form his own conclusions from the evidence, written and visual. We have not commissioned hypothetical reconstructions, the annotation of which, done properly, would take up quite a percentage of the text.

In this fourth book of the series Dr. McGowan deals with the development of ships between the year 1700 and 1820. Again, the book is of necessity centred on developments in Britain, but, as in all the other books in this series, the approach is nevertheless an international one. At this period especially developments in the merchant shipping industry and in naval affairs spread rapidly outwards from their country of origin.

As Dr. McGowan makes clear, the most important steps forward during this period were in the introduction of fore and aft sails into the classic three-masted square-rigged vessel which had emerged from the great revolutionary developments of the 1400s. The great innovation of this period was the widespread adoption and development of the schooner in the 18th century and it was of course the schooner which, as the next volume in this series shows, was in the end developed to the point at which she was the only type of merchant sailing ship built in the greatly changed world of the early 20th century.

Dr. McGowan is Head of the Department of Ships at the National Maritime Museum.

Basil Greenhill
DIRECTOR, NATIONAL MARITIME MUSEUM
General Editor

Preface

We are used to hearing that the wheel was the first great technological discovery by man. The first use of the wheel at sea may not have been as gigantic a leap forward, but it was certainly a most important step in the development of the ship, and one which made possible the precise manoeuvring so important to the discipline and effectiveness of a battle fleet. The wheel also made it possible to steer large vessels much closer to the wind without danger from jibing, and so make the most advantageous use of fore-and-aft headsails. Similarly, the wider application of the fore-and-aft sail to all types of vessel in the 18th century is another aspect of the constant struggle to improve the profitability of ships in any given trade. These are but two of the developments traced in this brief survey of the sailing ship in the 18th and early 19th centuries.

The examples of the coastal craft discussed are some of the more interesting of the vast numbers of different types of smaller vessels which made up by far the largest proportion of the tonnage of shipping that might be described as northern European in origin. Fishing vessels as such have perforce been omitted, although many of the rigs and hull forms were either adapted to fishing craft or else from them: thus the smack rig and the lugsail are dealt with, although without reference to fishing boats.

The hundred years leading up to the successful application of steam propulsion at sea was a period of continual striving to improve the sailing qualities of the ships available. If progress was slow it must be remembered that in a world where the rhythm of life was governed almost entirely by the natural seasons, radical change in any form was looked at askance. Even in the late 20th century, which in 50 years has seen technological and scientific advances of staggering magnitude even against the background of the 100 years before that, innovation is still often looked upon with suspicion. How much more understandable is it then, that in the 18th century, when people were not attuned to change, it should be accepted only gradually and piecemeal.

The wooden ship

The 18th century, which covers most of our period, is generally seen as a time of relative stability, when the pace of life was leisurely. Not until the last quarter could the contemporary tune 'The World Turned Upside Down' be written with any relevance, and it is hardly surprising that the story of shipping in this period followed the general historical pattern of the time. For nearly a hundred years there was little real change except in details. Then, towards the end of our period one can sense a hastening of the tempo.

The leisurely years of the 18th century, with the gradually quickening pace of the early decades of that following, saw the end of a period in the history of the ship which had lasted for nearly four hundred years. From the middle of the 15th century, when the development of the three-masted ship of the northern tradition had made trans-oceanic voyages a commercial possibility, until the first quarter of the 19th century, ships had changed remarkably little. They had grown in size, naturally, and they had become more efficient machines, but built on the same principle and with the same rigging, there was a general similarity that, say, Vasco da Gama would have recognised.

Ships were built of wood and powered by the action of the wind on sails made of flax canvas, on masts and yards supported by natural fibre rigging, usually of hemp. The whole structure continually 'worked' when at sea, because of the thousands of individual pieces of timber of which it was made up, and because it was subject to continually changing stresses.

By the early years of the 18th century the basic structure of the square-rigged ship had been com-pletely developed, particularly in rig, so that even the change to iron and steel hulls only encompassed details. The only innovation in rig came with the widespread use of the schooner in the 18th century. The greatest change in the construction of wooden sailing vessels came with the introduction of the huge three-, four-, five- and eventually six-masted wooden merchant schooners that thrived briefly two centuries later, during the 50-odd years from the American Civil War to the mid-1920s.

In considering the development of the ship in the Western World and particularly in Britain during the 18th and early 19th centuries it will be convenient to look first at the various warship types. The detailed records kept by naval administrators have survived when, almost invariably, those of the commercial companies have not. Consequently, it is convenient to use warships to establish a framework of the basic developments at sea within which the important variations introduced into commercial vessels may be more readily identified in the wider context.

In actual construction although not in design, the methods used to build both warships and merchant ships were so similar, for our purposes at least, to be as one.

In 1700 the design of the hull for a wooden warship, basically unchanged for nearly 50 years, could already have been called traditional. Even more so could the term be applied to methods of building which had evolved during the 15th century.

The first stage was to build a skeleton, the backbone of which was the keel, with its supporting keelson, ending in the stem at the bow and the sternpost at the stern. To this were attached frames, the ribs of the skeleton, which conformed to the desired shape of the hull. The whole was locked together by the planking outside and the ceiling (also planked) inside; by wales, great timbers which girdled the ship fore and aft round the frames, and by transverse deck beams running from the frames on one side to their fellows on the other. All these timbers were fastened with oak trenails and wrought iron bolts, some of which in a ship of the line could be 6 ft long. Such bolts were driven through holes drilled in the timber and clenched on the other side. A trenail was a peg usually made of oak, although other hardwoods such as beech were used, particularly in the 19th century. It could be as much as $2\frac{1}{4}$ in in diameter and 3 ft long.

The favourite timber was oak and, to the conservative mind of the English shipwrights and seamen, it had to be from the South of England, preferably from Kent or Sussex. This unabashed bigotry was not entirely unjustified, but it was also carried along by a patriotic fervour about the innate rightness of anything English connected with the sea that had been born with the exploits of Drake and Hawkins in the reign of Queen Elizabeth I and apparently confirmed by the legend of 1588. Not unnaturally it was also fostered by the landowners with an economic interest to promote. The Three Dutch Wars (1652–54, 1665–67, 1672–74) reaffirmed Britain's position as a major maritime power which, with occasional periods of complete primacy, was to last another 250 years.

The history of shipbuilding in Britain contains numerous and regular complaints of the dearth of homegrown timber that date from the reign of Queen Elizabeth I. The Navy Board had to compete with commercial yards; both had to compete with other demands. For example, throughout the 17th century much good ship timber was lost from the Weald of Kent and Sussex to the iron industry for fuel. Even though the demands of the end of the 18th century were partially met by the plantings of the later Stuarts, there was never enough timber, particularly compass timber, which provided strength in the grown curves. A typical 74-gun Third Rate of 1760 needed approximately 3000 trees, each of which would provide about 50 cubic feet, in modern terminology the equivalent in the United States of about 600 board feet.

Although English oak was the favoured timber for the main structure throughout most of the 18th century, elm, beech and fir were also being used. A few years later the Navy Board turned towards teak, with great success. In the 18th century, imported naval stores – oak timber and plank, fir masts, tar, pitch and turpentine – came largely from the Baltic countries, although as the century wore on, for political reasons, Britain took advantage of the expanding timber trade of the New England colonies. After the Revolutionary War of 1776 Canada became significant as a source of naval stores, a fact emphasised by the Treaties of Tilsit in 1807 between France and Russia and France and Prussia, which were intended to close the Baltic ports to Britain. It is an indication of the volume and importance of the trade in naval stores that although the Treaties made supplies from the Baltic problematical, each year the Royal Navy escorted to Britain convoys of more than 500 merchant ships bearing the vital supplies.

Britain's chief rival at sea, France, also favoured oak and as the difficulties of supply increased throughout the period, she also came to accept the same alternatives.

In Britain, however, there were also other proposals to combat the timber problem. Sir Robert Seppings, Surveyor of the Navy 1813–32, experimented with methods of construction by designing a Third Rate to be built with timbers of scantlings – dimensions – suited to a frigate but compensating for their lightness by doubling them up. He also introduced a method of diagonal framing which not only made the hull stronger but which also permitted the construction of much longer wooden hulls than previously. At the same time, a certain amount of ironwork, now available in quantities because of the beginnings of industrial expansion, was also used as knees and other bracing.

Model of a 60-gun ship *c* 1703. This model is remarkable in that it provides the earliest evidence of the introduction of the steering wheel. That it represents a transitional stage is demonstrated by the presence of the box immediately ahead of the wheel. Open on the forward side, the box was a kind of cupola from which the helmsman at the whipstaff on the deck below could communicate with the officer of the watch.

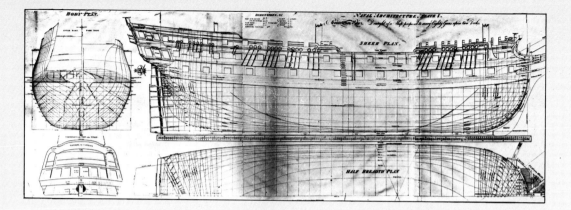

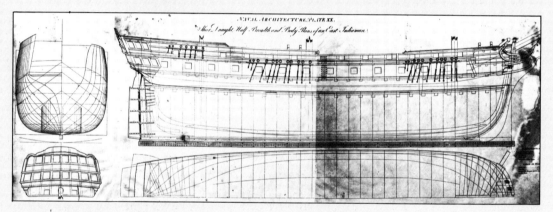

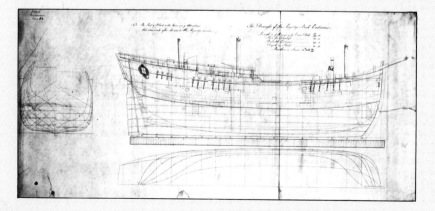

Warships of the northern tradition

By 1700 warships were designed – in Britain at least – by using a combination of drawings (draughts) and models. Although the illustration on p. 8 is nearly a century later, the drawings for an 80-gun ship are typical of one sheet of the six or seven usually drawn at that time for each warship or class of warship within its Rate. The draughts were technical documents largely for the use of the Surveyor of the Navy, who was responsible to the Board of Admiralty for the design of warships, and for his master shipwrights who were to build them. The models, built to scale and often in detail, were for the benefit of the members of the Board of Admiralty, most of whom could not read plans but, being seamen, could judge the proposed vessel's capabilities when, by means of the model, the plan was transformed into a three-dimensional 'drawing'.

The requirements of warship design were inevitably different from those for merchant ships. The need was ever that adopted as his tactical creed by an American general of the 19th century, whose avowed aim was always 'to get there firstest with the mostest'. The warship had to be a fast, stable gun platform; within the limits determined by her type and what was considered technically possible at the time, she was always a compromise between the ability to sail well and to carry as many and as heavy guns as were consonant with that ability.

The warship, therefore, was given an underwater body which permitted fast sailing and, above all, the ability to point close to the wind, *i.e.* to sail as nearly as possible in the direction from which the wind was blowing.

By about 1800 a well-handled ship of the line, with a clean bottom, was reckoned to be able to sail six and a half points off the wind – a matter of $67\frac{1}{2}°$, but in practice no two ships were the same. There were good sailers and poor sailers, and if a ship was truly one of the latter, the best handling in the world could make her only marginally better. A well-found frigate would make better time than a larger ship; a schooner or cutter make a faster passage still, hence their use as

The three ships were typical of their type and trade. The body lines should be read as contours – which is what they are. By convention, the body plan shows the lines viewed from the stern on the left hand side and from the bow on the right. Note the box-like shape of the hull of both the merchant ships at their widest point (mid-section), by comparison with the warship. Notice too that there are many more lines marking the changing shape of the warship hull, showing that not only is it finer in section at its widest point but also that it begins to shape towards bow and stern from much nearer the mid-section, *i.e.* giving a sharp entry and a fine run aft.

Comparison of the lines of 3 ships

	80-gun ship 1794	East Indiaman 1794	Bark *Endeavour* (formerly collier *Earl of Pembroke* 1764)
Length	182 ft (on lower deck)	165 ft 6½ ins (between perp)	97ft 8 ins (on lower deck)
Max beam	49 ft	42 ft	29 ft 2 ins
Depth of hold	21 ft	17 ft	15 ft 4 ins
Tonnage (burthen)	1955	1257	366

HEAD AND STERN VIEWS
OF A BRITISH SECOND RATE

Old Square Stern as built in 1758

Old Beak-head

despatch vessels. Notice, however, that actual speed has not been mentioned. Ships differed in their ability to sail at speed but this factor was subject to many variables, not the least of which was the state of the wind and sea. Fast passages were made because a ship could sail relatively close to the wind and in consequence had to sail fewer actual miles in tacking to make her desired course. The 'handiness' of a ship as it was called, the relative nature of which must be remembered, gave her captain another even more important advantage if she were a warship: the ability to gain the weather gage, *i.e.* get to windward of the enemy in a proposed action.

There were advantages and disadvantages in both the windward and the leeward positions. In the former, if the enemy was also disposed to fight, the commander could choose the moment and point of his attack because the enemy had no freedom of manoeuvre towards him. However, if the battle went against windward ship or squadron, it could not escape without first going by or through the enemy. On the other hand, if circumstances demanded a refusal of action or a withdrawal, the leeward ship or squadron could disengage more easily. A commander's choice of position – should he be granted it – would depend very much upon the circumstances, but it was important that he should have, in the handiness of his ship, the ability to make that choice and not have the tactical conduct of the battle dictated by the enemy.

The fine underwater body on which the vessel's sailing ability largely depended also had drawbacks, however. Below decks it produced awkwardly shaped spaces that were inconvenient to use and which in a merchant ship would have been uneconomical. In addition, the finer the lines the more careful the captain had to be if for some reason he found it necessary to take the ground, for a sharp vessel would fall over. Throughout the 18th century warships also showed a gradual flattening of the hull silhouette, so that the poop and forecastle were nearly similar in height above the upper deck, a trend consciously introduced by Sir John Hawkins in the 1580s and taken up again in the second half of the 17th century. This was also a matter of weatherliness, for the more the windage of the hull could be reduced, the better her sailing qualities were likely to be.

The shape of both bow and stern of major warships changed little throughout the 18th century. They were the weakest points in the construction of warships and every captain dreamed of being able to cross his opponent, raking the length of his gundecks with a rolling broadside as each gun came to bear. It was indeed a devastating manoeuvre. Although French frigates had been given the stronger round bow in the eighteenth century, it was Sir Robert Seppings who designed the first ships of the line with round bows and round stern, at the end of our period.

Seppings has already been mentioned as an original thinker in terms of warship construction. In 1803, while Master Shipwright at Chatham, he was ordered to cut down the 90-gun *Namur* to a 74-gun Third Rate. While considering the problem he realised the advantages to be gained by leaving the rounded, solid bow at the middle deck level instead of replacing it with the weaker square bulkhead culminating in the beakhead. This innovation would not only provide additional structural strength at one of the weakest points, but would also provide better protection from raking fire from ahead. The change was approved and was seen to be such a success on the *Namur*'s completion as a 74 in 1804 that the round bow was ordered on all new construction.

ROUND BOW AND SQUARE STERN
AS BUILT IN 1820

The new design for bow and stern. The new designs were not only inherently stronger in construction but also, as shown overleaf, they made for better defence, on the principle that every arc of fire should intersect those on either side.

CIRCULAR STERN BY SIR ROBERT SEPPINGS

ARCS OF FIRE AT BOW AND STERN

Stern

Bow

Middle Line

Given Sepping's imaginative approach to the problems of ship design, it is not surprising that he should then turn his attention to the equally vulnerable stern. His solution, predictably, was similar: the round stern was introduced by order of the Admiralty on 13th June 1817. It also provided a much needed additional strength, enlarged the space available to the stern battery and reduced the danger of being pooped, that is, overwhelmed by a following sea. At the same time, the projecting quarter galleries were removed, which considerably improved the ship's sailing qualities when working to windward.

The method of construction of warships – and of merchant ships too for that matter – was very much the same regardless of size. The greatest difference, naturally, lay in the scantlings of the timber used. In discussing rig, however, the same is not the case.

The differentiation in warships depended largely upon the number of guns carried, although small vessels were also categorised by rig. The largest ships in the navy were the ships of the line; that is, vessels powerful enough to take their place in the line of battle as used in major actions. The most powerful, the First Rates, mounted 100 guns and, by 1820, the increase in size permitted the largest to mount 120 guns. Such ships were very expensive to maintain at sea although their enormous firepower could make all the difference in a fleet action. There were rarely more than half-a-dozen First Rates and perhaps twice that number of Second Rates, which mounted 90–98 guns. Both of these classes carried their guns on three-decks. The only other three deckers were an unsuccessful design of 80–84 gun Third Rates, most of which were later reduced to two decks. The Third Rate was the standard ship of the line in that it was the most numerous and, apart from the 80-gun ships already mentioned, mounted 64, 70 or 74 guns on two decks.

As ships of the line gradually increased in size, although not necessarily carrying also an increase in armament, the 74-gun two-decker became the commonest Third Rate. Fourth Rates mounted 50–60 guns on two decks but after the middle of the 18th century, 50-gun ships were regarded as not powerful enough to stand in the line.

The ships of the line of the other major maritime powers were much the same as those in the Royal Navy, except that for a large part of the 18th century French and Spanish ships were, rate for rate, rather bigger than their British counterparts. The main consequence was that French and Spanish ships of the line, at least in the first half of the century, provided a more stable gun platform and on more than one occasion they were able to fight their lowest tier of guns in weather that rendered the British gun deck armament unusable because the latter was too near the waterline.

Fifth Rates mounted 32–44 guns on one deck except for the older 44-gun ships which were two-deckers. The Sixth Rate of 20–28 guns and all smaller warships carried their guns on one deck. Ships of the Fifth and Sixth Rates were cruisers and may be divided into two general groups. The larger cruisers, including the 50-gun Fourth Rates after they were excluded from the line, were most commonly used for escort duties and service in distant areas where enemy ships of the line were not so likely to appear. They were not really successful in that they were not powerful enough to pose a threat to enemy ships of the line but neither were they nimble enough to force an action upon smaller vessels. The other group was composed of frigates, the weatherly vessels bearing 28, 32 or 36 guns used for scouting and detached patrols. These ships were the 'eyes' of the battle fleet and no admiral of any nation ever admitted to having sufficient of them.

The frigate, in the commonly accepted sailing ship sense, appeared in the middle of the 18th century and it is arguable which country produced it first. In the Royal Navy the first large scale building of frigates was begun with the 28-gun ships of 1755, although it

Plymouth Harbour, Dominic Serres, 1722–1793. The fleet escorting a captured three-decker is seen going up to the Hamoaze anchorage before a south-easterly breeze. The prize leads the way, followed by the flagship. Drake's Island is in the centre of the picture, with Mount Edgcumbe in the background on the right. In the foreground the appearance of the smack's jib suggests that she is coming up into the wind to go about.

A boat was towed not only for convenience when it might be needed frequently, but also because towing allowed more working room on deck.

Shipping in light airs in the Thames Estuary, C. Brooking, 1723–1759. The merchant ship on the left of the picture is hove-to with a boat alongside. The wind has been spilled from her fore course, fore topsail and main topgallant sails by the simple expedient of lowering the yards on the lifts, to leave just enough sail drawing – the main and mizzen topsails – to counter the ebb-tide. The cutter on the left has the breeze dead astern and is said to be running; the similarly rigged hoy in the centre is seen on the port tack. Both these vessels demonstrate the enormous amount of canvas the cutter rig produced in relation to the hull size. The breeze is so light that the heel on both the hoy and the small lugger on the starboard tack is barely noticeable.

The single-masted lugger on the right is also running, but, with little canvas, will be making very slow progress against the tide. In the background two merchantmen are at anchor whilst a third drifts down on the ebb, perhaps to join them.

seems probable that they were based on the similarly armed *Unicorn* and *Lyme* of 1748. Subsequent experiments in frigate building followed, based on two main streams of development: one a design derived from British experience of small 20- and 24-gun ships; the other, including *Unicorn* and *Lyme*, derived from a French-built prize, the *Tygre*, but, significantly perhaps, a privateer rather than a naval vessel.

The size of this type of vessel gradually increased in all major navies during the remainder of the 18th century. By the 1790s 40-gun and 44-gun frigates, British and French, were in action. American frigates of 44-guns were particularly successful during the early months of the war with Britain (1812–14).

Perhaps the most famous of these, the *Constitution*, or 'Old Ironsides' as she is known, is preserved at Boston.

The increase in the size of frigates may be gauged by comparing the dimensions of the 44-gun *Constitution* with those of a typical 74-gun Third Rate of 1794.

USS *Constitution* (1797)	74-gun Third Rate (1794)
length (between perpendiculars) 175 ft	(gun deck) 176 ft
beam (greatest breadth) 43 ft 6 in	49 ft

This gradual growth in size and power, which was typical of all classes of warship in the 18th century and continued well into the 19th, was a natural evolution. Eventually each class might also have moved up a division in that the 50-gun frigates of 1820 could well have stood in the line as Fourth Rates in 1700.

All vessels mentioned so far, the First to Sixth Rates, were square rigged on all three masts, a fashion which by 1700 had already become firmly established as the standard rig for a three-masted ship. Before discussing rig, however, it is relevant to consider the two most important innovations concerning ship handling since the development of the three-masted ocean-going ship in the 15th century: the introduction of first, the steering wheel and then triangular headsails. Both occurred during the first decade of the 18th century.

It is surprising that in view of its great importance the advent of the steering wheel is so ill-documented. It was remarkable in the degree of control it gave the helmsman; not in the sense that he was able to move the rudder through a greater angle than with the 17th century whipstaff, but in that he could apply a far more sensitive movement to it because the mechanics had been improved. Relieving tackles on the tiller were still necessary in heavy weather but less so than with the whipstaff.

Despite the apparently total absence of documentary evidence, we are able to date the appearance of the wheel fairly precisely. One contemporary model, dated 1703, in the National Maritime Museum at Greenwich, shows a windlass in what later became the steering position on the upper deck. This windlass with a handle at each end is set with the barrel lying athwart the midships line, *i.e.* in the normal position for a winch or windlass. The idea was sound in theory but would rapidly have demonstrated its impracticability probably even at the model stage. It is obvious that if tiller ropes are to be attached to it, they must be led through a number of awkward angles since they themselves must first run almost athwartships to obtain any purchase on the tiller.

Clearly, the barrel had to be turned through 90° to lie along the midship line. But then the model also seems to emphasise another disadvantage which would give pause to anyone who has had anything to do with such contrivances. The small diameter of the barrel and the not much larger turning circle of the handle would make its use laborious at any time and a

A windlass steering control *c*. 1703. This drawing based on a contemporary model shows a stage in the search for a better means of controlling the rudder than could be provided by the whipstaff. The disadvantages of the windlass are manifest in the model and there is no evidence that it was ever so used.

near impossibility in anything like heavy weather. Worse, the speed of the rotating handles should the tiller and ropes 'take charge' would be lethal: the helmsman who only broke both arms in such circumstances would be lucky. However, once the barrel is turned to lie along the centreline, it is a simple step to see that a wheel fastened to the end would permit long spokes which would give the helmsman greater leverage and, therefore, greater control. What is more, from his point of view, the wheel would be turning across him rather than towards him, so that should the wheel 'take charge', his chances of avoiding injury would be much greater.

Whether such a device was ever tried, we do not know, but it seems unlikely because another contemporary model, also dated 1703, shows a conventional wheel. Man's naturally conservative nature is demonstrated by the inclusion in this model of the rowle, a fitting for the whipstaff where it passed through the lower deck. In the event, the wheel was quickly adopted for all large vessels and other countries followed suit.

The other major development was the introduction of the triangular headsail into ship-rigged vessels. The jib was adopted by the Royal Navy in 1705 and its appearance so soon after the development of the steering wheel can be no coincidence.

Throughout the whole of the 17th century the sails controlling the ship's head had been spritsail and the spritsail topsail set from the spritsail topmast, both square sails set well forward, which could certainly impart considerable leverage upon the bows. However, like most square sails, although they could produce immense power they were not capable of fine adjustment and in consequence the helmsman had to steer far enough off the wind to allow a safe margin of error to avoid jibing. This was of little real consequence as long as the method of steering, either by tackles or by whipstaff (or both), did not admit of fine control, but

once the steering problem had been solved and a capable helmsman was able to steer within much narrower limits, it became a practical proposition to sail close to the wind.

To the foretopmast staysail, which with the other staysails had come into use during the later years of the 17th century, a jibsail was added, set from a jib-boom extending from the bowsprit. These two fore-and-aft sails enabled the vessel to point much closer to the wind and they also had the additional advantage of being more easily handled than the square spritsails. Although on some of the larger ships the spritsail topmast was retained until the 1730s, it was probably only used under particular circumstances and as an alternative to the jibsail. It is difficult to see how the two could have been used together. After the spritsail topmast was removed, the spritsail topsail remained on the largest ships but was spread on a yard set below the jib-boom. The spritsails were used much less thereafter, except in light winds because of their tendency to drive the bow downwards. The braces and lifts for the yards were useful, however, for the support they provided for the bowsprit and jib-boom. In 1794 the flying jib-sail was added, set to the flying jib-boom. The fore and mainmasts carried course, topsail and topgallantsail. Royals, discarded after their use on the *Sovereign of the Seas* in 1637 were re-introduced as standard rig in 1779.

After 1730 the fore part of the lateen mizzen sail, *i.e.* that part forward of the mizzen mast, had been cut away, although the entire yard was retained, with the foot forward of the mast, giving the appearance of a gaffsail. In smaller ships this is what it became after 1745, but the ships of the line retained the long lateen yard until 1780. The change in the mizzen sail was undoubtedly the result of the greater use of staysails. The fore-part of the lateen blanketed the mizzen staysail and must frequently have fouled it. It was soon evident that it was not only unnecessary to have

Shipping in the Avon below Bristol, 1701, Jan van Beecq
c 1638–1722. Despite the somewhat fanciful scenery, the
60-gun ship broadside-on and the two 70-gun ships moored
ahead of her typify ships-of-the-line at this period. The
60-gun ship is presumably about let go her anchor, but she
appears to have a great deal of well-filled canvas considering
the lack of space available.

The neatly furled spritsail and sprit topsail can clearly be
seen. These were the last years of the richly carved and
decorated sterns. Because of the great expense, in 1703 an
order was issued prohibiting this extravagance. Alongside the
60-gun ship a small hoy awaits, with sails brailed up to take
the way off her. On the starboard quarter a cutter follows the
big ship in.

the whole of the lateen sail but also that in its original form it was an encumbrance. Thereafter, its evolution into a loose-footed gaff-sail was inevitable; this was the spanker. The driver was a rather larger version of the same sail, normally used in light airs only and always rigged with a boom. In 1810 the driver replaced the spanker as the mizzen sail, the boom becoming a permanent rig. Topgallant sails were set above the lateen mizzen but royals were not set on the mizzen mast until 1790. The square cross-jack (pronounced cro'jack), a sort of mizzen course, could also be set but it was only used when particular conditions favoured it. Studding sails which served to extend the width on each side of the normal sail were carried on the lower and topsail yards on the foremast and mainmast; topgallant staysails were added in 1773 and after 1801 main lower studding sails were not used. Staysails were set between the masts (see illustration p. 26–27). Originally triangular sails, all staysails except the fore staysail, the main staysail and the fore topmast staysail became quadrilateral in 1760.

Until about 1750 a number of smaller warships carrying 10–24 guns were classed as Sixth Rates. Thereafter, however, any vessel with fewer than 20 guns was classed as a sloop. The larger of these were ship-rigged, others were rigged as brigs or ketches. They were maids of all work as scouts and despatch vessels but because of their relatively heavy armament, they were probably most useful for inshore patrols, such as those required to keep the port of Brest under surveillance during the French wars. Not least in the achievements of these smaller cruisers, was the major part they played in the suppression of piracy in the West Indies in the early years of the 18th century, thus encouraging the development of the all important trade to the Caribbean and the American Colonies.

Of the many other small vessels used by the navy, we should perhaps consider three: the brig, the schooner and the cutter. It should be remembered that the duties of all these vessels, including the smaller sloops, were very much the same, with the exception of the cutter, which was more likely to be confined to inshore work. The brig, with its very similar sister, the snow, was widely used also as a transport. Square-rigged on both its two masts, it differed from the snow only in that the latter's gaff-rigged 'brigsail' was set on a separate trysail mast attached to but abaft the mainmast (see illustration p. 35).

The use of the schooner in the navy followed the pattern of the development of the vessel itself. The schooner rigged solely with fore-and-aft sails evolved on the Atlantic coast of North America out of the vessels used in the coastal trade between the colonies in the 17th century. The topsail schooner, on the other hand, developed later in the 18th century out of what were originally square-rigged vessels such as the brigantine, by the addition of a fore and aft foresail. The development of the two types of schooner is dealt with in the next chapter.

It seems probable that the navy first used the schooner in the West Indies in the early 18th century, in all likelihood during the operation of clearing out the buccaneers already mentioned. The schooners used would undoubtedly have been local craft hired or purchased for the specific service and it seems more than likely that almost all of the schooners employed in the West Indies or on the North American coast were of this type.

The first schooners actually belonging to the Royal Navy, as opposed to those hired for a specific service, appeared in the 1760s, purchased in North America. The most famous of these was, of course, the *Pickle*, which brought Collingwood's Trafalgar Despatch to Plymouth in 1805.

The cutter is interesting because of the enormous spread of canvas it carried and it should be remembered that the name referred to the rig; these generally excellent sailers are not to be confused with the relatively modern pulling cutter. A typical 18th century cutter would be about 72 ft long with a 25 ft beam, her huge gaff-rigged mainsail set to a 60-ft boom. By the middle of the century she carried a jib set on a long jibboom, with double topsails above a big running squaresail. The whole gave the cutter the appearance of being over-canvassed but this impression was belied by her performance. In fact, she was a beamy vessel, sitting deep in the water; a fast, weatherly craft, though not normally a good sailer in light winds. She was very well suited to coastal work in Northern Europe and was adopted in mid-century for widespread use in the British revenue service.

We have seen how, at the very beginning of the 18th century, the development of the steering wheel had a profound effect on the performance of all ocean-going vessels. Towards the end of the century another technical innovation, introduced in a cutter, was to have a similar effect upon designs of the very small craft. The sliding keel was designed for use in vessels up to the size of the smaller frigates. It was to be extensively used in schooner rigged merchant vessels in North America but its most widespread application was to come 150 years later when, as the centreboard, it was used in hundreds of thousands of small pleasure craft.

Captain John Schank, R.N., introduced the sliding keel to the formal European world of shipbuilding. It is impossible to say who invented the drop keel, as it was also called. Like many simple devices such as the wheel itself, the classic 'invention', it probably developed over a period of years. It certainly appeared, historically, quite independently, in places as far apart as China and South America.

It is almost equally certain that a form of the sliding keel was in common use in the Atlantic colonies of North America during the second half of the 18th century, for there are large stretches of shallow water along the coast from Long Island to Florida, the most extensive being Chesapeake Bay.

John Schank, a Master's Mate well known for his mechanical engineering ingenuity, was posted to North America in 1773 and it was typical of his character that he should quickly interest himself in the local craft. In 1774 he is known to have built, or caused to be built, a boat fitted with drop keels. By the mid-1780s when he was a Captain with a wide experience of local conditions and of sufficient rank to command respect for his opinions, Schank formally submitted proposals to the Admiralty for a cutter designed with sliding keels. In 1791 the *Trial* with three drop keels, was tested against a similar vessel built with a fixed keel. The *Trial* proved to be a great success and subsequently saw useful service on inshore patrols along the French coast. Larger vessels were also built, the most famous of which was the *Lady Nelson* in 1798. This vessel took part in the Matthew Flinders (*Investigator*) voyage of discovery to what are now Australia and Tasmania in 1802–3. The *Peggy*, a schooner with sliding keels now preserved in the Nautical Museum, Castletown, Isle of Man, also dates from this period.

Since man first kept any sort of boat in water for long periods a major problem that has bedevilled its efficiency has been marine growth. With a boat, of course, the remedy is simple: she is taken out of the water and scrubbed down. With a ship the same rules apply but the difficulties are very much greater. Consequently, for 250 years—since extended ocean voyages had become a practical possibility at least—ways had been sought to inhibit marine growth.

A second major cause for concern about the state of under-water ship timber was created by the ravages of the *teredo navalis*, which became a serious problem consequent upon the ability of ships to sail to the distant tropical waters, the original home of the 'ship worm'. Returning ships, infested with the worm, brought it to northern waters where, unhappily, it bred, for its favourite timber seems to be oak.

Model of the *Bellona* 74-guns. This model, finely finished
even by Navy Board standards and of an unusually large
scale, was built for Sir Charles Middleton (later Lord
Barham), when, as Controller of the Navy, together with the
First Lord of the Admiralty, Lord Sandwich, he successfully
persuaded King George III of the necessity and effectiveness
of coppering the fleet. Almost certainly the model used to
demonstrate the case, this is the first contemporary model to
show coppering.

Throughout the 17th century different remedies had been tried in attempts to solve both these problems, but unsuccessfully. For most of the 18th century the generally ineffective answer to the *teredo* was to sheath the hull with additional planking laid over a coat of tar mixed with hair. This additional 'skin' could be relatively easily stripped off and replaced.

Although the first experiments with copper sheathing seemed to have been effective, certainly in keeping the hull clean, it was found that the galvanic action of the copper on the iron fastenings of the planking and main timbers had caused corrosion of dangerous proportions. For nearly ten years little more was done but in 1775 experiments were begun to find a means of protecting the iron bolt heads.

A solution had apparently been found by 1778 for within the next four years virtually the whole fleet was coppered. The bolt heads were driven flush with the planking and protected from the copper by a layer of heavy waterproofed paper. In the event, this was not as sufficient protection as had at first seemed the case, but it did play a crucially important role as an intermediate stage. By the time serious defects appeared in 1783 the value of coppering had been clearly demonstrated, both in terms of inhibiting marine growth and in protection against the teredo. The final solution was to use non-ferrous fastenings in the form of hardened bolts made of copper and zinc. Other countries were quick to follow suit, particularly when the sailing qualities of weed-free copper-bottoms had been demonstrated in action. The use of copper sheathing became almost universal, and variants of it, *e.g.* copper mixed with zinc, to produce more durable metal, were used as long as wooden ships were built.

We have seen during the 18th century a steady improvement in the design and efficiency of warships. Apart from the major technical innovation of the wheel and triangular headsails at the start of the century, changes were in detail rather than sweeping. One important factor which must always be remembered when comparing warships with merchant ships – which can rarely be done like with like and so must be considered with some care – is that despite manning problems generally, warships always had a large complement of men. Merchant ships, on the other hand, were designed to show a profit and since labour has always been a costly commercial item, crews were invariably kept to a minimum.

Timber barks, Samuel Scott, 1710?–1722. The most striking
feature of this painting is the capacious bulk of the Danish
timber ship in the right foreground with its plain stem and
bluff bows; another, by convention, is shown stern-to on the
left of the picture, although she is shown wearing a British
ensign. The artist has quite unnecessarily exaggerated the
ponderous appearance of these vessels by depicting all the
men on the Danish ship in half-size. The characteristic bow
feature, the simple and totally unadorned stem, is clearly
shown.

It is a still day; as the crew of the Danish ship make ready
for sea, a boat lays out a kedge anchor to help her into the tidal
stream.

The problem of terminology for 18th century rig is amply
demonstrated. Scott painted these vessels calling them barks,
quite correctly according to contemporary usage, but both are
ship-rigged.

Foreign-going merchant ships

At the beginning of the 18th century the merchant ship of northern Europe had reached a stage where it could be developed in its own right, without the need to make concessions towards being pressed into service as an auxiliary warship in time of need. In most trades, in fact, it was unnecessary to arm the ships with ordnance of any sort. Because they were exceptions and accounted for only a small proportion of the total tonnage, it is convenient to deal with the armed ships in the far distant trades first.

The most famous of these trades was that carried on by the East India Companies, Dutch, French and English, and the comments concerning their ships are relevant, to some degree, to the ships used in the trade with the West Indies and the Levant.

These were defensible merchant ships, frequently armed with more than 30 guns—a most necessary precaution as they traded in waters eight or nine months' sailing time from home and far from the protection of warships. They had to be able to protect themselves against foreign vessels whose owners resented competition in a lucrative trade, and also against merchant captains from their own country for whom monopoly rights meant little.

Of between 400 and 500 tons burden with a keel length of about 140 ft, these large East Indiamen resembled Third Rate ships of the line from a distance and could give a good account of themselves, except against a warship or if taken by surprise and boarded by pirates.

Their size enabled them to stand heavy weather and they were invariably well found, not only in terms of the ship herself but also the crew, for the profitable trade enabled the company to pay the best rates and obtain prime seamen. If they were to fight, however, they needed to be faster and above all more weatherly than merchant ships for which tactical manoeuvring was no consideration. For this the East Indiamen needed finer lines. They were by no means as sharp in their underwater section as were warships but their shape gave them sailing qualities which could not be matched by normal cargo vessels.

In terms of the development of the ship the East Indiaman was in fact an aberration and of no great importance except in the service for which it was designed. It was after all a merchant ship, the chief requirement—indeed the only requirement—of which is to make profitable voyages for its owners. Yet the peculiarities of the East India trade saddled it with the two great economic disadvantages of a warship: a large crew capable of handling the ship whilst manning at least one broadside of guns, and under-water lines which, however advantageous in sailing, made stowage more difficult and inconvenient and, therefore, more costly than was normally profitable. It was, of course, only the vast profits of the East India Company that made such ships capable of economic operation.

However, the great bulk of shipping lay in trades where the realities were much harsher. The East India Companies flourished in something of a false world; other merchants flourished because they were forced by economic laws to make their ships more efficient and therefore more profitable. This was achieved in two ways, by carrying larger cargoes and employing fewer men.

By far the greatest expense to the shipowner has always been the cost of manpower, and the relationship of manpower to the efficiency of any merchant ship may best be expressed in terms of tons burden, *i.e.* paying cargo, per man employed on board.

The ability of a ship to carry a large cargo depends entirely upon the shape of the hull. Remembering that the speed of a ship is a function of her length on the waterline, length is important chiefly in its relation to her beam. Much more important to her carrying capacity is the shape of her transverse section. The fine lines which gave warships the necessary handiness and weatherly qualities, produced awkward spaces which not only made stowage difficult but also reduced the volume of space available. As we have seen, this mattered less when the cargo was valuable, in relatively small quantities, such as those carried by East Indiamen. For bulk cargoes with a high stowage factor, *i.e.* occupied a great deal of space but which were modest in value, the amount of accessible hold stowage was crucial.

The ideal hull shape, purely from a cargo-carrying standpoint, would be an oblong box, but such a shape would be quite difficult to push through water. However, if the ends and the bottom are shaped appropriately—just enough to ease its passage through the water—the box becomes a cargo-carrying vessel of moderate manoeuvrability. This concept had been the legacy of the Scandinavian-influenced Dutch vessels of the 17th century and it is interesting to see how it was thrust upon an almost unwilling body of shipwrights and shipbuilders in Britain. It is also interesting to note in passing how close to this ideal naval architects have come in the second half of the 20th century by the use of specially designed bows and slow-running engines driving a large propeller.

English shipbuilders in late Tudor and Stuart times were concentrated on the Thames and the ports of East Anglia, such as Ipswich, Yarmouth, Aldeburgh and Woodbridge. These builders were famous among the seafaring nations of Europe for the excellence of

HEIC *York*, Thomas Luny, 1759–1837. The *York* is shown running easily under topsails into the Madras roads. Two other Indiamen lie at anchor, that on the extreme right, the smaller type of about 300 tons.

their defensible ships. Stoutly built, suitably armed and reasonably handy or 'nimble' according to the vernacular of the day, they were fairly sought after – witness the visit of Venetian merchants to England to buy ships in the 1620s. In the circumstances, it is not surprising that the English merchants were also content with such vessels.

However, the picture was changed following the three Dutch Wars, particularly the First Dutch War 1652–54. The most common Dutch merchant vessel was the *fluit* or flyboat as it became known in England. These ships were not armed and to a large extent had the characteristics of our aforementioned, shaped oblong box. Bluff-bowed and flat-floored, they were ideal carriers, with the additional advantage that their relatively flat underwater section amidships enabled

them to take the ground without undue harm – a considerable advantage in a time when deep-water berths were confined to a very few major ports.

It has been estimated that more than 1200 of these vessels were captured between 1652 and 1654, which, sold off relatively cheaply as prizes of war, flooded the English market. The capacious flyboat quickly proved its value and, fortunately for the newly enlightened shipowners, supplies of them were renewed during the wars of 1665–7 and 1672–74. The light, however, was not seen by the established ship-builders who would not – surely, rather than could not – adapt themselves to produce the new form of unarmed merchant vessel. Even when the flyboats captured during the Third Dutch War were approaching the end of their working life the yards of

Model of HM bark *Endeavour*, 1768. This beautifully finished and accurate model of the *Endeavour* demonstrates the typical hull form used for the various bulk cargo carriers. *Endeavour* was built at Whitby as the *Earl of Pembroke*, a collier, and the similarity to the Danish timber barks (see p. 22) is striking, even though the view is quite different . It will be noticed that like them the *Endeavour* was ship-rigged. In her case however, the apparent anomaly is simply explained. She was rigged as a ship because that was the standard rig for a three-masted vessel in the navy; she was called a bark because a ship was a captain's command and James Cook was at that time a lieutenant. That particular term was probably used to solve the problem of how to classify her because she was bought into the Royal Navy as a collier-bark.

East Anglia were unwilling to supply the type of hull that had become economically vital to the bulk cargo trades in coal, timber and flax. As a result, because the shipowners would not be denied and went elsewhere, the yards of East Anglia declined, never really to recover. With the exception of the Thames yards, which were assured of orders for Indiamen and the defensible ships that were required, shipbuilding in England moved to the North-East where the demand for bulk carriers was greatest among the collier owners and the timber merchants trading across the North Sea to the Baltic.

By 1700 the shipbuilders of Whitby, Scarborough and ports on the Tyne and Tees had developed their own version of the flyboat, but one that was perhaps rather larger. The North Country 'cat', as the type became known, was the ideal, general purpose merchant ship of its day. Rather bigger than the flyboat, the cat-built vessel became the standard for the bulk carrying trades, especially coal and timber. Many of these cats were of 250–300 tons burden, that is they were large vessels for the early 18th century.

Mention has been made of the Scandinavian influence on the development of the flyboat, but there was also a more direct influence from the Baltic on the bulk-carrying vessels developed in the North-East. The term cat itself seems to have been Scandinavian in origin, for Norwegian cats were described as being used occasionally in the coal trade. These large vessels also had the hull characteristics of the flyboat but, pole-masted, they were rigged without topgallant sails and so were economical in manpower.

In 1700 the dividing line between two and three masted ships seems to have been at about 50–60 tons, with the exception of those in the coal trade. However, although two-masted colliers were often much larger than 60 tons, the big cats of about 300 tons were three-masted and rigged with spritsail and spritsail topsail, with course, topsail and topgallant sails on the fore and main masts, with lateen mizzen and mizzen topsail, and staysails.

The centres which had traditionally supplied British ships were not only threatened from England's North East coast, however. Shipbuilding in the Colonies of British North America had flourished from the middle years of the 17th century. By the Restoration in 1660 the colonial shipyards were supplying all the shipping the Colonies needed for themselves and were making inroads into the provision of ships for the transatlantic trade. By the accession of William and Mary in 1688, roughly half the ships in trade between

Throughout the 18th century, as the steady increase in trade lessened the dangers of loss of revenue while ships waited for cargoes, or by ships sailing with only part cargoes, merchant ships grew in size.

There was a considerable increase in the number of ships built of 100–300 tons burden, but until the middle of the 18th century little or no increase in the size of the largest ships. Thereafter, East Indiamen which for the first half of the century had been between 400 and 600 tons, increased in size and by 1820 several had been built of more than twice this tonnage. In the Baltic trade until about 1750 the largest vessels had been of about 350 tons.
By 1770 new ships needed to replace old ones were nearer 500 tons, with a few vessels in the timber trade over 100 tons larger still.

However, the gradual increase notwithstanding, it must be remembered that by far the largest proportion of both ships and tonnage in foreign trade came from vessels of less than 200 tons until early in the 19th century.

We have seen the increase in size of the larger merchant ships. At the same time the tonnage at which vessels were rigged with three masts rose sharply.

Leaving the coal – and probably the timber trade too – aside for a moment, it will be recalled that in the first years of the 18th century vessels were rarely two-masted above 60 tons. By the 1730s the dividing line came at 80–90 tons and it had risen to 140–150 tons by the Seven Years War (1756–63). By the time of the American War of Independence 17 years later there were a few two-masted ships of more than 200 tons.

The three-masted ships included most of those in excess of 200 tons burden and certainly all those of 300 tons and more. Of these the larger vessels of more than 400 tons were ship-rigged. That is to say, square sails were carried on all three masts: course, topsail and topgallantsail on the fore and main masts, lateen (after mid-century gradually becoming a spanker) with a square topsail above it on the mizzen mast, and jibsail, forestaysail and 'tween mast staysails, with studding sails on the fore course, fore topsail and the main topsail.

The development of the ship rig had occurred as a logical progression, with the natural tendency to give the vessel as much power as possible as hulls became larger in the 17th and 18th centuries.

During the middle years of the 18th century, however, a modified form of ship rig was introduced into vessels for which speed was not essential, almost certainly as a means of economising by a reduction in the number of the crew.

During the 17th and 18th centuries the term 'bark' was used fairly indiscriminately, as also was the term 'ship', much as the word 'vessel' is today. Increasingly, however, from the middle of the 18th century onwards one finds vessels described as 'bark-rigged' or 'ship-rigged' until, in the next century, the adjective was dropped. A vessel square-rigged on all three masts became a ship and a vessel rigged with no square sail on the mizzen became known as a bark, perhaps transferred to barque by 19th century Romanticism in Britain, although North American usage continued with the earlier spelling.

We can only offer conjecture as to why each type of rig was given that particular name. Undoubtedly ship-rigged was so called because it was the more common—just as the word 'ship', as a general description, was more widely used than 'bark'. Bark-rigged is much less certain in origin.

Given that the reduction of sail area could be introduced economically only in a trade that was constant in its demand—*i.e.* for the same reason that sailing ships were still commercially profitable in the wool, wheat and coal trades of the late 19th century—it is logical that the bark-rig should have been introduced into the cat-built colliers of the coal trade on Britain's East Coast. We have already noted the example of the pole-masted Norwegian cat. But how were the vessels built on the North East coast described immediately prior to the introduction of the bark-rig? As cat-built colliers? Cat-built ships? Cat-built barks? Each is possible but given the eventual corruption of any name that is not instantly and easily pronounced, surely cat-bark is a far more likely description than cat-ship or cat-collier. There are indeed documents of the 1760s in which they are described as cat-barks—at a time when the term is hardly likely to be applied to rig for the simple reason that the particular form of rig, with no squaresail on the mizzen mast, was not at that time sufficiently well established. Hence bark-rigged came to refer to the economical rig that had its origin in the cat-barks.

The effect of the economies made by carrying more cargo per vessel or by a reduction of manpower because of a modification in rig, or both, can be measured quite simply in terms of tonnage of paying cargo carried per man in the crew. This economy of scale can be effected in large vessels because, of course, there is a minimum number of hands required to work

TABLE A
Average tons per man, British ships entering London

from	1686	1726	1751	1766
Hamburg and Bremen		10.1	12.2	14.3
Holland		8.8	10.8	11.8
France		8.4	10.6	10.9
Spain and Portugal	7.9	9.1	11.5	12.6
Norway		20.3	21.6	20.0
Riga and Petersburg		13.5	18.1	19.4
Jamaica	8.7	8.6	11.4	14.4
Other W. Indies	9.3	9.8	10.5	13.5
Virginia and Maryland	9.8	10.8	13.0	15.6

even the smallest vessel suited to a given trade, but whilst the capacity of the vessel might be increased by, say, 50 per cent, the new, larger vessel would not require an increase of 50 per cent in the crew to work it. The following tables, taken from Ralph Davis, *The Rise of the English Shipping Industry*, clearly indicate that the number of tons per man increased significantly during the first 70 years or so of the 18th century.

It will be seen that the first trade involving English ships in which this efficiency was demonstrated was the Norway trade, where large vessels were required for the bulk cargoes of timber and where sharp competition was already provided by highly economical rigs such as that already noted in the Norwegian cat. It is apparent that because of this competition the optimum size of ship in this trade crewed by the minimum number of men was reached early in the 18th century. A few very large vessels increased the tonnage per man to 21.9 (TABLE B) in 1766 but the overall figure for that year is very similar to that of 40 years earlier. The difference between the figures for the Norway trade and the remainder for 1766

(TABLE A) is a reflection of the generally smaller vessels used outside the timber trade.

By 1766, in the other trades, the number of tons per man had increased by an average of about 43 per cent. We do not have to look far to see the reasons for this increase but, although they are difficult to prove conclusively, the circumstantial evidence is considerable.

Professor Davis suggests that the increase in efficiency occurred because of a major development in merchant ship design of which we are unaware, but, whilst it is true that relatively little is known of merchant ship construction in the middle of the 18th century (apart from East Indiamen), compared with the vast body of documentary evidence on naval construction for the period, it is inconceivable that any such development could have occurred without its having left a single trace. Hull design *per se* is not a factor in this evidence of greater economic efficiency, although hull size is contributory.

Insofar as technical innovation caused the increase in tons per man, it was surely in the adoption of the wheel for steering and the increasing awareness of the value of the fore-and-aft sail on large vessels. It will be recalled that the wheel was first introduced into warships in about 1703 with the jibsail closely following. It is reasonable to assume that once the effectiveness of the wheel and the jib had been proven, merchant ship owners followed suit. It is arguable, however, that the reasons why both the Navy and merchant owners adopted these innovations are different, or at least have different emphasis.

The Navy was primarily concerned with efficiency of sailing. That it needed fewer men to handle the jib than the spritsail topsail, or that the wheel was less demanding upon manpower because it was less tiring than the whipstaff, and being more efficient demanded less use of men on relieving tackles, was convenient and no doubt welcome. But there were always hands available on a warship because of the extra men

ABLE B Average tons per man, in ships of various sizes	Tons: 300 and over	200–299	150–199	100–149	50–99	under 50
Hamburg and Bremen		18.9	15.7	13.3	11.4	
Holland			16.5	13.1	10.6	8.1
France				14.8	10.9	6.9
Spain and Portugal		16.5	14.5	12.4	10.4	7.0
Norway	21.9	19.0	17.0			
Riga and Petersburg	21.9	17.5	15.1	13.3	11.4	
Jamaica	16.0	14.8	12.2	10.5		
Other W. Indies	15.8	14.5	13.5	11.0	7.9	
Virginia and Maryland	18.7	16.6	13.3	12.5		

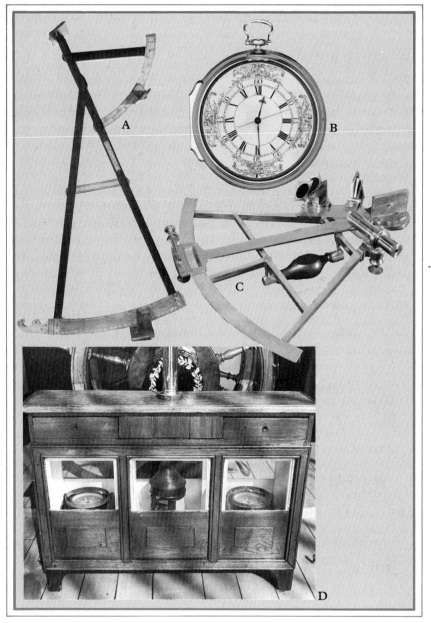

(A) Backstaff, 1720. Until an efficient chronometer was available the principle behind all ocean navigation lay in latitude sailing calculated by celestial observation. The standard practice was to steer for the appropriate latitude and then run down the easting or westing to make a landfall.

First introduced in the late 16th century, the backstaff relied on the shadow cast by the sun. It was improved by John Flamsteed (1646–1719), the first Astronomer Royal.

Although superseded by Hadley's reflecting quadrant in 1731, the backstaff remained in use for much of the 18th century.

(B) John Harrison's chronometer, 1759. There was no satisfactory method of calculating longitude until a reliable marine chronometer had been developed. Prompted by a competition instituted by the Board of Longitude, John Harrison (1693–1776) built a number of chronometers, the fourth, the dial of which is illustrated, ultimately being deemed successful in 1773 after a number of trials. The H4 is in the form of a large pocket watch some four inches in diameter, in marked contrast to the larger, clock-type mechanism of his earlier chronometers.

The Harrison chronometers are in the National Maritime Museum at Greenwich.

(C) Sextant *c* 1870. The introduction of John Hadley's reflecting quadrant (1731) meant that for the first time accurate astronomical measurements could be taken from the heaving deck of a ship at sea.

John Campbell's sextant was evolved from the quadrant, using the same principle but extending the arc to enable measurements of up to 120° to be taken.

required not only to serve the guns but also to handle the sails when speed of sailhandling could make the difference between life and death. To the merchant owner and captain, although greater efficiency of sailing was useful, it is unlikely that passage times could be improved upon sufficiently to allow an additional voyage in a season, the only real commercial incentive. Much more important was the opportunity that the wheel and jibsail gave him to reduce the crew – even by one or two men. This change took place gradually, with the larger ships being affected first, others being adapted as the modifications proved themselves. It must be remembered that we are concerned only with ships in the deep sea trades and not even the smallest of these. Crew reductions were possible only in large vessels; those of less than, say, 100 tons already had crews so small in number that reduction for the reasons under discussion was hardly possible.

The gradual natures of these changes – Blanckley's *Naval Expositor* of 1750, for example, explains the use of the whipstaff, suggesting that it was still to be found in use at that time – also accounts in part for the apparently continuous improvement in tons per man for the first 70 years of the 18th century. Similarly, the gradual development of the lateen mizzen sail into a gaff rigged spanker or driver and the introduction of the bark rig, aided economy in manpower in the later

(D) Box-binnacle. This was the standard form of binnacle used on board both naval and merchant ships throughout the period covered by this book. A compass could be seen from either side of the wheel, the lamp in the centre compartment providing illumination at night. The box binnacle shown is on board HMS *Victory*.

(right) *Sheldrake* Packet, N. M. Condy, 1810–1851. The *Sheldrake* is seen reaching in under topsails. She is barque-rigged but notice the brailed up trysails that have been added to the fore and mainmast. These, with the staysails, were important in improving the performance to windward; they were not, however, considered suitable for very large vessels such as East Indiamen and ships-of-the-line. They continued in use into the present century; the Aland barque *Fred* built as late as 1920, was equipped with a main trysail.

On the left of the picture another barque-rigged merchant ship lies hove to, the Master perhaps talking with the tug on her starboard side.

part of the century. Neither is likely to have occurred early enough to affect the tons per man figures for 1766.

But, of course, technical innovations in rig did not merely enable owners to man the same ships with a reduced crew. Rather, the owners were encouraged to keep the same crew for much larger ships which, together with the expanding nature of trade, was an important factor in the gradual increase in merchant ship size throughout the century.

Particularly effective in this regard were the increased used of staysails and the development of more efficient reefing arrangements. Whilst neither of these permitted an absolute reduction in the numbers of crew required, they undoubtedly improved the performance and allowed the use of larger hulls with no increase in manpower. At the same time, because economic conditions encouraged the construction of larger ships, owners pressed to the limit the size of vessel that could be handled by a crew of any given number. In this they were no doubt assisted

unwittingly by the manning problems which beset the Navy.

In all, the eight wars in which Britain took part during the period 1700–1820 occupied 58 years and they were sufficiently spread out that in 120 years there was no period of peace longer than 13 years. In wartime, when the Navy required large numbers of men and warrants for the press were issued, there was a shortage of prime seamen. No trade was exempt from the press, with the occasionally disregarded exception of the East India Company. As a result, merchant ships were frequently sent to sea undermanned – but the fact remains that they went to sea. That they were undermanned is undeniable; the point is that owners continually had evidence before them of what could be achieved with a minimum of hands in a crew and there is no doubt whatever that the lessons were learned well.

So far we have considered only the three-masted vessels – those of more than 200 tons, but by far the greatest proportion of merchant tonnage in the 18th

(left) A coal brig, Edward Gwyn, fl. *c* 1769? This rather primitive water-colour drawing of an 18th century collier brig shows the rig clearly, particularly how large the boom and gaff driver mainsail had become.

(right) Snows *c* 1750, C. Brooking, 1723–1759. By the middle of the 18th century, almost the only readily distinguished difference between a brig and a snow was the trysail mast fitted abaft the main mast. The painting follows the convention of showing two views of the same vessel; in this instance, however, the artist has shown one at anchor and the other sailing away on the port tack.

century consisted of ships smaller than 200 tons. In 1788 five out of every six vessels owned and registered in British ports were of less than 200 tons burden.

As Britain had the largest single merchant fleet at that time, with a greater proportion of large ships than any other nation, it is fair to say that in terms of world tonnage the proportion of merchant ships under 200 tons was considerably greater than 83 per cent.

Most of this ocean-going tonnage was made up of brigs and snows. Both the brig and the snow were economical in manpower in that they carried two masts only. Not surprisingly, this economy was increased in the same manner as that of the ship: by increasing the hull size whilst still retaining the same number of sails. Whilst both these rigs demonstrated their ocean-going ability, of the two the snow was more commonly used for the trades involving long voyages and the brig more usually found in the coastal and short sea trades. This is, of course, a generalisation to which there were numerous exceptions. Certainly it is true, however, that the largest two-masted vessels tended to be rigged as a snow, *i.e.* fully square-rigged on both fore and main-masts with a trysail mast and trysail abaft the mizzen.

The reasons for this are not clear but may have been that the snow rig bore rather more canvas than the brig rig. For example, the former carried a main yard on its mainmast—the aftermost of its two masts, whereas the brig was rigged with the lighter cro'jack yard, the sail of which was less often used than the square mainsail of the snow. The mainsail of the brig, on the other hand, was the boom and gaff driver, a fore and after sail that increased in size as the 18th century wore on. Brigs also made much use of the main staysail which, in the ship rig—to which on its two masts the snow more closely conformed—was of less value because it was usually blanketed by the square mainsail or main course.

It will be seen that although the brig was clearly a square-rigged vessel it made greater use of, and was

more dependent for power upon, its fore-and-aft sails than either a ship or a snow. However, this is not as might be thought a further example of the development of the fore-and-aft sail; rather is it a reminder that the brig evolved from the brigantine, which was essentially fore and aft rigged on the mainmast. Nevertheless, we have seen an increasing appreciation of the value of the fore-and-aft sail during the 18th century, an awareness that was shown in two ways. On the one hand there was the greater application of the fore-and-aft sail to the square-rigged ship in the form of triangular headsails, staysails and the replacement of the rather clumsy lateen mizzen by the gaff spanker, and, at the close of the century, the gaff and boom driver sail. On the other hand, there was the development of the schooner rig, where the concept was totally different: a rig based on the fore-and-aft sail wherein the square sail, if it was used at all, was used in a solely auxiliary role.

One should perhaps consider briefly the differences in fore-and-aft sails and square sails. The square sail was suspended from a yard which lay at right angles to the ship's keel and in order to move the vessel in any given direction, it received the wind on one side only. To go ahead, unless the bottom was clean and the ship a good sailer, the wind had almost to be abaft the beam at least, the yards being trimmed to make the best use of a wind not dead astern. Such sails were ideal on long ocean passages with strong, constant winds but they needed men aloft to set or hand them (take them in).

The fore-and-aft sail lay basically on a line with the ship's keel and to send the ship forward it could receive the wind on either side. It had three advantages over the square sail. First, it could move the ship ahead with the wind some degrees forward of the beam; second, it did not normally require men to go aloft and was, therefore, more economical in manpower; third, it was much more effective than the square sail in light winds unless the wind was right astern. The chief advantage gained by the increasing use of fore-and-aft sails in combination with square sails therefore, was the ability to sail closer to the wind. The vessel that was primarily fore-and-aft rigged could sail far closer than a square-rigged vessel. There were two disadvantages of the former; first, in our period at least, it was only suitable for relatively small vessels because fore-and-aft sails for big ships had to be enormous and required large crews to operate them. The huge wooden schooners in use in the early 20th century were economical to run solely because of the use of a donkey engine to provide power for sail handling. Second, when running before a heavy wind and sea there was some danger of being overwhelmed because of the heavy booms and sails far out over one side.

Rigs dominated by the fore-and-aft sail had been well known in the 17th century but only in small craft which normally worked in coastal waters. The schooner was the first deepsea vessel to be so rigged and although it was used by the navies of the world as a despatch vessel and for patrolling confined waters, the chief importance of the schooner was as a merchant ship, a cargo carrier. Just as we have seen that the introduction of fore-and-aft sails into square-rigged vessels enabled the tonnage to be increased by a greater proportion than the additional number required in the crew, so the vessels that were essentially fore-and-aft rigged held a built-in advantage in economy of manpower over vessels of a similar size that were square-rigged. However, the economical advantage was strictly limited because even by the end of our period, in the first decades of the 19th century the largest merchant schooners were rarely more than 100 tons.

With the exception of the brig and the brigantine, the basic difference between a schooner and square-rigged vessels is in the purpose of the fore-and-aft sails. In the latter they are used largely to deflect bow or stern, *i.e.* as balancing sails and also as staysails, to lift the bow and so make the power of the square sails, which drive the ship forward, more effective. In the schooner, however, the fore-and-aft sails not only have the same two functions, but they also provide the main driving force.

As demonstrated briefly in an earlier chapter, the schooner had dual origins, each quite distinct from the other but which led to the development of the same type of vessel, the rig of which has the characteristics outlined above. In our period, it should be noted, almost all schooners were two-masted.

Brigantine sloop *c* 1745, John Clevely, 1747–1786. The term sloop in this case indicates the vessel's rating in the Establishment, *i.e.* that it is a Commander's command. She is seen hove to with the fore course clewed up and the fore topsail backed, the yards on the main mast all braced fore and aft to minimise the effect of the wind.

The interesting point is that she seems to be bilander rigged. The lateen yard has been lowered, but the extent of the furled sail dropping from the lower arm of the yard could only come from a settee sail.

The fore-and-aft schooner – the so-called American schooner – evolved from the small two-masted gaff-rigged vessels used in colonial American waters in the 17th century. This rig probably had Dutch origins but appeared in America both directly from Holland and, indirectly, from Britain. The triangular headsail was also known in European and American waters in the 17th century, although only on small one-masted craft. But, put the two together, the triangular headsail with the two gaff sails, and the resulting rig, also used in the shallop, becomes that of the schooner.

We cannot be sure when this new rig first appeared, although the evidence suggests that it was early in the

A schooner with a view of New York, J. T. Serres, 1759–1825. American schooners with square topsails were less common than purely fore-and-aft rigged schooners, and John Serres, unlike his father, Dominic, was never a professional seaman. As a representation of an early 19th century topsail schooner hove-to, the general impression is good although rigging details are missing.

17th century. Given the evolutionary nature of its development, a more precise date is hardly to be expected. Unfortunately, the origins of the unusual name applied to it are totally obscure, although the word 'schooner' first appears in 1721 in a manner which suggests that it needed no explanation, *i.e.* it was already a well known term. Regardless of the origins of either the rig or its name, however, the fact remains that the schooner represents one of the two major developments in sailing rig since the appearance of the three-masted ship in the 15th century, the other being the crucial introduction of the wheel and triangular headsails.

So far, we have been concerned solely with the fore-and-aft schooner, but the efficiency and handiness of these vessels were not lost upon owners and masters—frequently one and the same person—who were, for various reasons, wedded to the use of the squaresail. By the middle of the century, or soon after, similar vessels were appearing with typical schooner fore and main-sails but which also had square topsails on one or both masts. It is interesting to note that a number of contemporary drawings show square topsails in use on the main mast only. This was presumably to avoid the tendency, produced by using a square topsail on the fore mast, to drive the bow downwards and so lose speed. The topsail schooner, as this type became known, almost certainly originated in European waters, and, certainly, this type of schooner was more popular there than on the coasts of North America. It was not, however, merely an American schooner to which topsails had been added.

The evidence of contemporary illustrations suggests strongly that the topsail schooner is an example of the 18th century phenomenon already noted in three-masted ships: the tendency towards an increased use of fore-and-aft sails. In this case, however, the rig is two-masted and the change was almost certainly concentrated on the brigantine, for we have already seen

Northfleet Hope, Thomas Dutton fl. 1858–97. Depicting a blustery day in the Thames Estuary just above Gravesend, the picture shows an East Indiaman, perhaps rather larger than life, although the small craft are well drawn. The two hoys each have the foot of the mainsail hoisted to enable the skipper to see ahead; the spray at the bow of the sailing barge on a broad reach suggests that the wind is against the tide. The ferry, with its easily handled rig, is of interest, as are the small boats, among them what appears to be a sprit-rigged peter-boat, taking passengers off the East Indiaman.

how her larger sisters, the brig and the snow, developed in both size and rig, including, of course, an increase in fore-and-aft sails, particularly in the former.

The smallest of the trio, the brigantine, was similar in size to the schooner and, therefore, susceptible to the influence of the new rig. It seems probable indeed, from the forward position of the foremast in 18th century illustrations, that many of the topsail schooners of that time were re-rigged brigantines. The real evidence, however, would seem to lie in pictures of the early topsail schooners which show them with a main staysail. That this sail would have been inconvenient, if not quite impossible, to use with the fore gaffsail is evident and it was soon dispensed with. The fact remains that it was at first seen as part of the topsail schooner's rig and this can only be because it had always been a feature of the brigantine rig. Further, all the evidence of the trends in the 18th century point towards the introduction of more fore-and-aft sails into a square-rigged vessel. There is no evidence at all of an increased use of square sails in a rig that was basically fore-and-aft.

Throughout most of the 18th century the topsail schooner was common in American waters but it was gradually ousted by the fore-and-aft schooner which, by the early 19th century, dominated the American coastal trade. In this, climate was an important factor. Fore-and-aft sails were more efficient than square sails in the light winds often to be found on the Atlantic coast of North America. Further, the use of square sails required men to work aloft, which the winter temperature often made impossible; fore-and-aft sails could be handled from the deck. Inevitably, economic factors were also important. The fore-and-aft schooner tended to be rather smaller in size and was certainly more simply rigged than the topsail schooner. It was in consequence cheaper to build, to rig, to maintain and to man. Capital costs and labour were hard to find in the North America of the 18th and early 19th centuries.

On the other hand, there was more readily available money in England for the capital outlay on the topsail schooners that were more appropriate to the heavy weather conditions likely to be found on the British coast. As a result of these economic circumstances we find that the topsail schooner was commonly used in the transatlantic trade, the fore-and-aft schooner being used mainly in the American and West Indies coastal trade. These are inevitably generalisations to which exceptions can certainly be found; there is ample evidence, for example, of transatlantic passages by fore-and-aft schooners, so that there is no question of their capability. All the same, it seems that the topsail schooner rig was more suited to the transatlantic trade just as surely as it was less well suited to North American coastal conditions – on the East coast at any rate. It seems, therefore, that there may have been the same sort of general relationship between the use of the two schooner types as existed between the snow and the brig.

We have seen how the innovations of the 18th century had a considerable effect on the development of cargo-carrying vessels both in size and rig. But these were the large vessels – even though the vast majority were of less than 200 tons – in foreign trade. Although our interest has been centred upon British and American vessels, the types were common to all the trading nations of the Western World. Equally common to each trading nation was the existence of a very large fleet of smaller vessels with a variety of rigs, which carried the life blood of the country's economy in the coasting trade.

Coastal and short sea traders

In the 18th century there were no railways, and in even the most economically advanced countries only a mere skeleton of good roads linked the main towns. For the rest, such roads as there were belied the name: rutted tracks that were a sea of mud in any wet weather.

In circumstances of such limited means of communication, access to the sea and the coasting trade was all-important. The small sailing vessels of all kinds provided bulk carriage of goods like coal, timber, salt, stone, wool, *etc.*, to the ports for distribution to the hinterland. By this means the navigable rivers became arteries carrying the life-blood of the area. By our modern concepts the term 'port' is itself misleading, conditioned as we are to thinking of deep-water berths at permanent wharves with adjacent warehouses. A port is still a legally defined area, including the main harbour and all its creeks and beaches, although the latter are no longer used for loading or unloading. In the 18th and 19th centuries the creeks and beaches were used for these purposes. Deep water berths were available at a bare handful of ports in the whole of Great Britain and the coastlines of the continent of Europe and North America were no better served. Far more common was the situation where the loading or discharging generally took place on an open beach with a falling tide. This entrepôt trade formed the backbone of the national economy, but in the inaccessible areas on the coasts, say, of Cornwall, Wales and Scotland, of Brittany, Jutland and on the north coast of the Baltic, villages literally depended upon the coastal trade, not merely in economic terms but often for their very existence.

Scotch smacks, E. W. Cooke, 1811–1880. By the early part of the 19th century regular sailings were made between Leith and London to provide a passenger and cargo service. Typical cargoes were salmon to London, and beer, seen here being loaded from the barge, to Scotland. Notice the doublings to protect the planking from damage by the flukes of the anchor as it is hauled up and catted.

The greatest part of this 18th century coastal trade was carried in small vessels of between about 20 and 50 tons using a variety of rigs. The largest vessels were often the square-rigged ketches, brigs or brigantines and, occasionally in the later years of the 18th century, schooners. As we have seen, there was a tendency to increase the size of the vessels throughout the period and this applies equally to those in the coastal trade, so that by 1820 the largest vessels were nearer 100 tons.

However, although the general trend was towards larger vessels, local requirements often made it necessary to retain small craft—the tidal range, for example, could make a small vessel necessary not only because of the limited depth of water but also because of the limited time available for unloading over a dry beach.

By far the most common rig was that of the smack, a term usually applied to the sloop rig, *i.e.* a one-masted vessel rigged fore-and-aft with jib, forestay-sail, boomless mainsail and gaff-topsail. It was equally used, however, of the small vessels that were cutter-rigged, *i.e.* similar to that of the sloop but with the addition of a square topsail. It is very difficult to talk of rigs in any but the most general terms and this is particularly true of the small vessels. The word of the owner and master—the terms were often synonymous in the coasting trade for the latter was usually a shareholder—was law on the subject of his vessel. She was rigged as he wanted her to be and her rig was what he said it was. To illustrate this in the simplest way, his smack might or might not carry a square topsail but regardless of whether she did or not, she was very likely to carry a large, square, running foresail that was rigged for any voyage with the wind abaft the beam for long periods as, say, on a run up channel from Looe to Southampton. The bowsprit might be fixed but frequently, and especially if the vessel had much river work where there was little room to manoeuvre, it was not. If the owner did not care for a running bowsprit

A Fresh Breeze off Cowes, George Chambers, 1803–1840. The Portsmouth wherry was commonly used as a ferry between Portsmouth and the Isle of Wight.

In the foreground the passengers are enjoying the run down the Solent towards Cowes in the early afternoon. Ahead of them the larger form of the wherry is seen with a small mizzen lugsail set in addition to the fore staysail and spritsail. On the left of the picture a brig is seen eastbound.

A collier-brig discharging into carts *c* 1800, J. C. Ibbetson, 1759–1817. A common enough sight until the end of the 19th century, this little brig, her size well illustrated by the waiting carts, is seen discharging her cargo of coal across the open beach.

he might well dispense with it – and the jib – altogether, using the fore staysail as his only headsail, in the manner of a hoy – but I daresay he still called her a smack.

The hoy, the sturdy little maid-of-all-work whose appearance seems so typical of the small vessels of the 18th century, normally had the simplest and most economical of rigs: a fore staysail and a boomless gaff mainsail, although in certain trades a square topsail was also used. Like the smack the hoy, varying in size from about twelve to fifty tons, was found in every facet of the coastal trade, carrying such diverse cargoes as salt, stone, coal or vegetable produce.

The hoy was also the vessel most commonly used for the coastal passenger traffic of the day. On the River Thames they plied between London Bridge and the lower reaches, responding to a hail from the shore if their services were required. The shout of 'Ahoy' to attract the attention of another vessel may well have originated in this practice.

As trade prospered in the 18th century its concentration upon London created cargo-handling problems that could only be solved by the eventual building of a system of closed docks. In the intervening period ships had to wait at moorings for their turn to be unloaded into the small vessels which landed the cargoes at either the original legal quays between London Bridge and the Tower of London or at one of the sufferance wharves, which, as the name implies, were additional wharves specially licensed to receive or ship certain goods. (There is an excellent model illustrating this point in Gallery 11 at the National Maritime Museum.)

For much of the 18th century hoys were used for this work, especially in loading and unloading the larger ships such as the East Indiamen that were rarely brought above Blackwall and never beyond Deptford. However, this work became increasingly the job of the barges which developed their own characteristics as the volume of trade increased and their role expanded.

At the beginning of the 18th century Thames barges were scow-shaped, flat-bottomed rectangular boxes with sloping bow and stern. In the centre of the latter was set a fixed rudder, known as a budget, to help keep the barge straight. For the most part barges were not rigged but merely worked the tides, steered, with some difficulty one would think, by the use of a sweep or large oar at the stern. Such barges were known as lighters. Those barges that were rigged had a simple square sail and a large square rudder; they still used the tides, of course, but had, in addition and depending upon the wind, a greater degree of movement.

The shallow draught of the barges, together with their economical use of manpower and so cheapness of operation, enabled them to dominate this type of work. With so crude and basic a craft to begin with, it was obvious that improvements could be made without prejudice either to its carrying capacity or to its cheapness. The earliest pictorial evidence of a Thames barge in a recognisable 'modern' form dates from the 1760s and it seems probable that soon after mid-century the basic improvements had been made to the hull: the bow was curved inwards slightly, producing in the swim-head a rounded effect that was not only aesthetically more pleasing but was also more convenient in handling. Although the established hull form changed little over the next 150 years, for a long time it was seen with a number of different rigs. The square sail was replaced by the more efficient fore- and aft-sail – often, but not always, in spritsail form and a fore staysail was added. To assist sailing to windward the Dutch practice of using a leeboard on shallow draft vessels was adopted. A large paddle-shaped board was attached to each side of the barge on a pivot, that on the leeward side being lowered to prevent the drift to leeward, rather in the manner of a modern centreboard.

Collier discharging, E. W. Cooke, 1811–1880. A collier-brig
is shown discharging her cargo into lighters which were
propelled by a sweep over the stern. On her starboard bow
the hoy *Speedwell* of Wapping under forestaysail only is about
to pick up her mooring. Astern of the collier is a sprit-rigged
peter-boat.

(left) Chalk barges, E. W. Cooke, 1811–1880. These 'stumpies', so called because for ease of working above the bridges they carried no topmast, carried the simplest of barge rigs. Note the swim-head. The master of the inboard barge has protected both himself and his oiled sails from the chalk dust with old canvas.

(below) The Thames at Redriffe, Thomas Whitcombe, 1752–1827. Redriffe was the vernacular corruption of Rotherhithe. The view shows Limehouse Reach looking downstream, with St. Anne's parish church in the distance.

In Mr. Woolcombe's yard a vessel is seen in frame, whilst next to it another is prepared for launching. The rigged ship, also wearing her ensign in honour of the occasion, and with her main topmast housed, is the *Prince George*. Built in 1789, the *Prince George*, 300 tons, was in the West India trade, employed between London and Jamaica.

The small vessel causing the wherryman concern has the hull and rig of a Dutch sloop. In the distance a smack beating up from Greenwich Reach has just rounded Cuckold's Point.

For nearly a century the Thames barge was rigged in a variety of ways. Many were cutter rigged with boom and bowsprit; others without either were rigged in the manner of a hoy. As in the smack rig the permutations were endless. Eventually, economics triumphed although it was not until well into the 19th century that the spritsail rig in one or other of its forms became that most widely adopted for the barges. Efficiency for its original purpose, with economy of manpower, was the great characteristic of the Thames barge thereafter. The key to this economy was that all the gear could be handled from the deck by one man, for the great spritsail was never lowered but brailed in to the mast. The single mast, stepped well forward, left plenty of room for a large and easily used hatch. These vessels could carry 50–60 tons or more and,

with a crew of rarely more than two, had a far higher tons per man ratio than their erstwhile competitors, the hoys. Lighters, of course, were still used in abundance but their use was inevitably limited in scope. Eventually, the larger topsail barges, together with the ketches and schooners, were to squeeze out altogether the ancient but heavily built and labour-intensive hoy.

Shallow draught vessels that were also roomy and economical to run fulfilled a similar function in other parts of Britain. They were not in any way developed from the Thames barge because they had quite different structural characteristics and appeared contemporaneously with it. The similarity occurred in the service they performed and the conditions in which they worked. The Tyne keel, short and beamy, was essentially a river coal-carrier and not often rigged. The Humber keel, on the other hand, was very similar to the Thames barge – closer in appearance perhaps to the hull of the barge of later years since she was

Greenwich Reach, E. W. Cooke, 1811–1880. The smack on the left has the mainsail partly scandalised so that the skipper can see ahead where a topsail schooner is just passing a sloop-rigged barge.

essentially double-ended, with bow and stern similar in shape; the swim head was never used. She was, however, square-rigged with both main and topsail; she was also fitted with leeboards.

The local function of the Norfolk wherry was similar to that of the barge although she tended to be used more for passenger traffic than Thames barges ever were. Her lines were altogether finer and for work in deeper water she was usually fitted with a false keel. Her single sail was gaff-rigged.

Two other areas which were growing in importance in the 18th century, the Severn and the Mersey, as the ports of Bristol and Liverpool increased in size, also produced vessels doing the same job as, and somewhat akin to, the Thames barge.

The Severn trow was a vessel with its origins in the late-Middle Ages, at which time it was probably constructed in a similar fashion to the medieval cog. By the 18th century it had long since developed into an orthodox skeleton-built vessel whose main characteristics were flat bottom, with round bilge and bluff bows, high bulwarks at both stem and stern – the latter with its distinctive D shaped transom – and an almost total absence of decking.

Square-rigged, as a single-masted vessel, it carried mainsail and topsail. With two masts arranged ketch fashion, *i.e.* mainmast forward of amidships, the mizzen was lateen rigged. As in the case of the Humber keel she was commonly without a headsail. The trow remained square-rigged until the second half of the 19th century, the change in rig coinciding

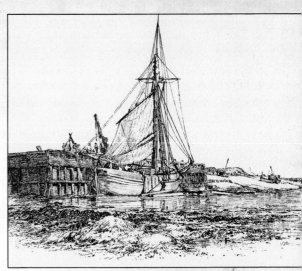

Off Ramsgate Harbour, Thomas Whitcombe, 1752–1827. These two smacks of the early 19th century demonstrate how an almost unbroken surface of sail could be achieved in a well found vessel. The light yard for the running squaresail is lowered to reduce its resistance to the wind.

The painting shows clearly function of the shrouds: in the smack on the right, on the port tack, the weather shrouds are bar taut with the strain; on the other vessel the lee shrouds, bearing almost no weight, are slack.

(left) Billy-boy, E. W. Cooke, 1811–1880. A vessel peculiar to Yorkshire, the Billy-boy had all the characteristics of the bulk carrying craft of the North-East coast. Her great cargo capacity and her ability to sit easily on the mud at low water are evident. Notice the leeboards to facilitate her use in shallow water. These cutter rigged craft were among the largest clinker-built vessels.

roughly with the widespread introduction of decked trows, both converted and new built, for similar reasons. As steam tugs and lighters gradually began to dominate the canal trade the trow was forced to compete for traffic in the more open waters of the Severn estuary and the Bristol Channel. The change to fore-and-aft rig was, as always, undoubtedly influenced by the need to economise in manpower. At the same time, however, away from the confined waters of the canal when the winds were contrary, the trow lost its traditional secondary means of propulsion, man or horse haulage. For the trow to compete with other small craft in estuarial waters a change to fore-and-aft rig was essential.

The last of these regional craft under consideration, the Mersey flat, was a creation of the mid-18th century, for until the 1720s the Mersey, Irwell and Weaver were barely navigable. As the name implies, these vessels were flat-bottomed and both bow and stern were similar in shape.

Unlike the Thames barge, however, although it had a hard, rounded bilge, the flat was not built with a hard chine. These vessels also began by having a single squaresail but by the early 19th century were often rigged with a spritsail and a fore staysail.

These then were the barges of the 18th century and they played a very important role in British commerce for roughly 200 years. The characteristics common to all were three in number: shallow draught with a virtually flat bottom, a large carrying capacity, and a simplicity of rig that reduced to a minimum the manpower required. In the preceding chapter the increased ratio of tons per man has been demonstrated in the sea-going vessels but the number of tons per man carried in barges at the end of our period in the 19th century, was far greater than in any of the vessels discussed previously.

The sailing barge was not a coasting vessel of any importance during our period, although this was the time when its potential was becoming apparent.

Dutch galiots, E. W. Cooke, 1811–1880. This drawing demonstrates the distinctive hull form of Dutch coastal craft, but the pole masts were not peculiar to Holland. The brig in the background is probably a collier.

During the 18th century the greatest proportion of coastal trading in British waters was carried on by smacks, and these hard-worked little vessels undoubtedly retained a very large part of it throughout the 19th century.

Rather larger than the smack was the square-rigged ketch, a two-masted vessel of considerable antiquity which, because of its greater size, had developed over the centuries with many characteristics of the square-rigged ship. It must be remembered, of course, that when writing of ships of the 18th century any terms referring to size are strictly relative. The ketch, larger than the smack, was one of the smallest square-rigged vessels. At the beginning of the 18th century the rig generally consisted of fore staysail, course and square topsail on the main mast, cro'jack yard with square topsail and lateen sail on the mizzen.

Quite early in the century a jibsail was added and although the course was no doubt carried as a running sail, the mainsail was a fore and aft spritsail. By mid-century this had often become a standing gaffsail and the lateen mizzen a spanker. Soon after, in the 1760s, the mainmast also carried a topgallant sail and, by the end of the century, two or three jibs were common. The addition of a main topgallant sail is indicative of an increase in the size of the vessel. The trends that have already been noted in other vessels during the period obviously also applied to the ketch: a move towards improving performance to windward by the increased use of fore-and-aft sails and a general increase in hull size. Early in the 19th century the square topsails gave way to gaff topsails, presumably to economise in manpower, perhaps because of the wartime shortage of trained seamen. With this change the ketch became a completely fore-and-aft rigged vessel, with the occasional exception of the square running sail which was rigged only when convenient.

The ketch was widely used in the British coast and short sea trades in which it was joined in the second half of the 18th century by the topsail schooner.

Blackwall Reach 1829, E. W. Cooke, 1811–1880. A variety of rigs is seen coming up on the flood tide with little wind. In the foreground is the simple rig of a Dutch schuyt, followed by a sloop, two or three colliers and a sailing barge. On the extreme left another barge with every stitch of canvas set is moving slowly downriver past an anchored galiot. In the distance, nearer Blackwall, a ship is being towed out by an early paddle tug.

It will be recalled that in the previous chapter the different characteristics of the two types of schooner were discussed and that in fact the fore-and-aft schooner was rarely used in British waters. They were known, of course, and doubtless a few that had sailed the Atlantic were operated by British owners; the point is, however, that none—or very few—vessels were rigged as fore-and-aft schooners for British owners. The question was unlikely to arise, for a British owner who preferred the fore-and-aft rig almost invariably used a ketch, a vessel with sailing capabilities very similar to those of the fore-and-aft schooner and one with which, as we have seen, he was already familiar. For similar reasons, of course, the ketch was rarely used in North America, the owner naturally preferring the schooner, a craft he already knew well.

The vessels dealt with so far in this chapter have been largely British in origin but the same sort of story could be told about the coastal trade of any of the maritime nations of north-western Europe. Not surprisingly, since the essence of overseas trade is communication with people of another country having similar interests, rigs and types of vessel, including the names given to them, are common to several countries, a point well illustrated by a few examples.

In the shallow waters of the Netherlands, a country whose influence is so often seen in types of rig and hull forms, the hoy was as common a sight as on British coasts. On the Dutch hoy, however, a jib was set and the mainsail was sprit-rigged. By the end of the 18th century a small sprit-rigged mizzen was also often carried. Dutch sloops had a sprit-rigged mainsail and a fore staysail only. The *galiot* and the *howker* were rather larger but had the same shape hull with its readily identifiable characteristics: broad beam, almost double ended, with bluff apple-cheek bows and a marked sheet. The *galiot* was really a single-masted vessel although a small driver with boom and gaff was occasionally set from a mast right in the stern.

Beaching a Pink at Scheveningen, E. W. Cooke, 1811–1880. In this splendid painting the artist has caught the sense of orderly confusion evident at such a moment. In the stern three men at the capstan are hauling the pink's head into the wind, the cable leading forward and then to the anchor already laid out. Two others grapple with the mainsail; forward three men with boathooks are also endeavouring to prevent her being blown broadside onto the beach, whilst overhead the loosed jib cracks in the wind.

On the starboard quarter, the beam trawl rests on the bulwark.

Ashore a small anchor is being carried up the beach and will be used, with the capstan, to haul the pink stern-first up onto the beach.

She carried a jib, staysail, a yard for a running square-sail, square topsail and a loose-footed mainsail on a standing gaff. The two-masted *howker* might be likened to the ketch. By the end of the 18th century she carried as many as three jibs or perhaps two jibs and a square spritsail below the bowsprit. The square-rigged mainmast might have a mainsail, topsail and topgallant sail, or just the first two; on the mizzen was set a driver and from the topmast a square topsail. By this period, of course, the ketch was rigged with a fore-and-aft mainsail. The other major difference was that the *howker*'s mainmast was in one piece, *i.e.* it was a pole mast.

The Swedish version of this vessel, the *hukare*, was in fact rigged in the manner of an 18th century ketch although the smaller types carried no mizzen topsail and, instead of the spanker, set a driver from boom and gaff.

Another Scandinavian vessel of this type was the Baltic galeas, so called to distinguish it from the earlier Mediterranean craft of the same name with which it had no connection. The Baltic galeas almost certainly originated as a square-rigged vessel but by the middle of the 18th century it was essentially rigged in the manner of a fore-and-aft ketch. With two jibs, a fore staysail and gaff-rigged main and mizzen sails, in its development towards total fore-and-aft rig it was some 40 to 50 years ahead of its British counterpart, the ketch. Only the square main topsail remained as the last evidence of its square rig origins. Inevitably this too was later replaced by a gaff topsail.

The Dutch herring-buss or *fluit* had the typical bluff-bow, flat floors and almost exaggerated sheet of most Dutch vessels. They were not double-ended like the galiot, however, but had a high narrow stern. Each of the three masts was square-rigged although only the

Boier in a Fresh Breeze, George Chambers, 1803–1840. The *boier* was originally a double-ended vessel which dropped out of use in the late 17th century. The name was later applied to the round sterned craft often used for pleasure sailing, depicted here. She has just come round onto the port tack.

On her starboard bow a *fluit* lies at anchor, her scandalised mizzen sail showing just enough canvas to keep her head to wind. To port, a small *bezaanschuit* with its ancient canoe-shaped hull is also rigged with staysail and spritsail.

main carried a topsail. A jib and a driver were often, but not invariably, set. As its name implies, the herring buss was originally a fishing vessel but its capacious stowage made it a most useful trader.

The *bilander*, Dutch in origin, gradually went out of use by British owners in the 18th century although it was still used by the Dutch. The hull was typically Dutch but the two-masted rig was unusual. A square spritsail was set beneath the bowsprit and both masts were square-rigged with course, topsail and topgallant sail on the foremast. The mainmast was rigged with top sail and topgallant sail but the mainsail was a settee sail, that is, set like a lateen but quadrilateral rather than triangular. This rig was somewhat clumsy, however, and was driven out of the British coastal trade by the ketch and later the topsail schooner. The name is interesting and should be pronounced to rhyme with islander, for, in Dutch (bijlander) it means literally a vessel to sail 'by the land', *i.e.* a coaster.

Finally, two French vessels complete the examples of European coastal traders. The *bugalet* was a small two-masted square-rigged vessel used mainly by Bretons. It carried one, or perhaps two, jibs, a foresail, mainsail and main topsail. The other example, the lugger, is not necessarily French in origin although its origins are obscure and it was certainly widely used on both sides of the Channel. However, it may be argued that this extremely efficient rig was brought to its highest pitch by the seamen of Brittany and Normandy.

It seems most probable that the dipping lugsail was developed, perhaps in the Mediterranean, out of the lateen sail, a hypothesis given some support by the generally similar method of handling the two sails, in small boats at least. Despite the ancient use of another version of the lugsail by the Chinese, the European lugsail seems to have been developed independently.

Lugger *c* 1800. This contemporary model of a French lugger demonstrates the considerable area of canvas this type of small craft could carry. They were good sailers on most points but excelled in working to windward. The immense leverage exerted by the jib set on a long bowsprit and by the mizzen set to a bumkin made them highly manoeuvrable.

Note the uncommon practice of rigging the fore and main topmasts abaft the lower mast, which was held by some to improve the sailing qualities under certain conditions.

The lugger was widely used as a fishing vessel, particularly line fishing for mackerel and drift net fishing.

It was also used to great effect as a privateer, particularly from Brittany, during the Napoleonic Wars.

It may be that this most efficient sail was introduced to northern waters by French seamen whose links with the Mediterranean are obvious. The fact remains that until about the middle of the 18th century, the lug sail was confined to small open boats.

This early use in small boats also suggests that the lugsail might have been influenced by experiments with a square sail braced further round than usual, something unlikely to occur either by accident or by design in a larger square-rigged vessel. Whatever the origin of the sail the second half of the 18th century saw a widespread development of the larger lugger and by the end of our period, the early 19th century, genuine three-masted luggers were in use. However, the two-masted lugger was the most common form, with occasionally a small mast set right in the stern carrying a small balancing sail, the foot of which was spread by a bumpkin. With two jibs, foresail and foretopsail, mainsail and maintopsail – all lugsails, *i.e.* on yards slung at one third of their length and lying roughly in a fore-and-aft line – the lugger was efficient on all points of sailing. Unfortunately, the difficulty of handling large dipping lugsails limited the size of such vessels; as a result, their trade was lost to the ketches and schooners. Probably the most famous – and perhaps best handled – luggers were the *chasses marees*, the privateers, large Breton-manned, which preyed upon British commerce in the Channel during the wars of 1792–1815.

We have seen that, certainly in terms of rig and almost in terms of size, the wooden sailing ship had reached the limits of its evolution by the early 19th century. The last of the great wooden line-of-battle ships built in mid-century strained the ingenuity of designer and shipwright alike, so near to the limits of wooden ship construction had they come. The largest wooden ships ever built, the great American and Canadian schooners, came at the end of the century but they were to have no descendants. Their story is told in book 7 of this series, The life and death of the Merchant Sailing Ship 1815–1965. Like the steel four-masted barques which developed in the same years, they were profitable for a brief period, but the day of the wooden sailing ship had long since gone.

A Baltic Galeas *c* 1760. This attractive illustration on a piece of Liverpool ware depicts well one of the most commonly found cargo carriers in the Baltic Sea of the 18th century. There is a striking similarity between this vessel and the galeas drawn in Chapman's *Architectura Navalis Mercatoria* of 1768, which, however, is shown with a main topsail only.

Bibliography

Baugh, David. *Naval Administration 1715–1750*, Navy Records Society Vol. 120 (London, 1977).

Blanckley, T. R. *The Naval Expositor*, (London, 1750).

Carr, F. G. G. *Sailing Barges*, (London, 1951).

Chapman, F. R. *Architectura Navalis Mercatoria*, 1768, facsimile reprint, (London, 1971).

Clowes, W. Laird. *The Royal Navy, a History*, 7 vols. (London, 1897–1903).

Davis, Ralph. *The Rise of the English Shipping Industry*, (London, 1962).

Knight, R. J. B. 'The Introduction of Copper Sheathing into the Royal Navy 1779–1786', *Mariner's Mirror LIX*, 1973 pp 299–310.

Landstrom, Bjorn. *The Ship*, (London, 1976).

Lees, James. *The Masting and Rigging of English Ships of War 1625–1860*, (London, 1979).

March, E. J. *Spritsail Barges of the Thames and Medway*, (Newton Abbot, 1970).

Moore, Alan. 'The Snow', *Mariner's Mirror II*, 1912 pp 38–43, 176–180.

Moreton, Nance, R. 'Ketches', *Mariner's Mirror II*, 1912 pp 362–370.

Morris, E. P. *The Fore and Aft Rig in America*, (London, 1927).

Smith, P. C. F. (Editor), *The Journals of Ashley Bowen (1728–1813) of Marblehead*, (Salem, Mass. 1973).

Steel, David. *Rigging and Seamanship*, (London, 1794).

Naval Architecture, (London, 1805).

Model of the *Trial* cutter, 1791. This model demonstrates Captain Schank's design for a cutter with sliding keels. The contemporary hull model has been restored and the rigging is modern.

Index

THE SHIP

The first seven titles in this major series of ten books on the development of the ship are: 2. *Long Ships and Round Ships: Warfare and Trade in the Mediterranean, 3,000 BC–500 AD*, by John Morrison; 4. *The Century Before Steam: The Development of the Sailing Ship 1700–1820*, by Alan McGowan; 5. *Steam Tramps and Cargo Liners: 1850–1950*, by Robin Craig; 6. *Channel Packets and Ocean Liners: 1850–1970*, by John Maber; 7. *The Life and Death of the Merchant Sailing Ship: 1815–1965*, by Basil Greenhill; 8. *Steam, Steel and Torpedoes; the Warship in the 19th Century*, by David Lyon; and 9. *Dreadnought to Nuclear Submarine*, by Antony Preston.

The remaining three books, which are to be published in 1981, will cover: 1. Ships in the ancient world outside the Mediterranean and in the mediaeval world in Europe (to the 15th century), by Sean McGrail; 3. The ship, from *c* 1420–*c* 1700, by Alan McGowan; and 10. The Revolution in Merchant Shipping, 1950–1980, by Ewan Corlett.

All titles in *The Ship* series are available from:

HER MAJESTY'S STATIONERY OFFICE
Government Bookshops
49 High Holborn, London WC1V 6HB
13a Castle Street, Edinburgh EH2 3AR
41 The Hayes, Cardiff CF1 1JW
Brazennose Street, Manchester M60 8AS
Southey House, Wine Street, Bristol BS1 2BQ
258 Broad Street, Birmingham B1 2HE
80 Chichester Street, Belfast BT1 4JY

Government publications are also available through booksellers

The full range of Museum publications is displayed and sold at
National Maritime Museum
Greenwich

Obtainable in the United States of America from Pendragon House Inc.
2595 East Bayshore Road
Palo Alto
California 94303

HMSO
BOOKS

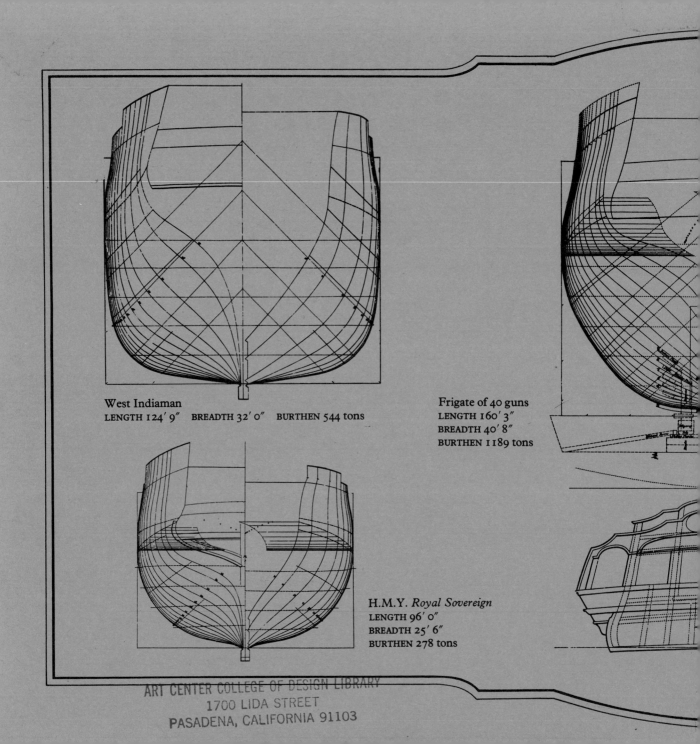

West Indiaman
LENGTH 124' 9"   BREADTH 32' 0"   BURTHEN 544 tons

Frigate of 40 guns
LENGTH 160' 3"
BREADTH 40' 8"
BURTHEN 1189 tons

H.M.Y. *Royal Sovereign*
LENGTH 96' 0"
BREADTH 25' 6"
BURTHEN 278 tons